A Crabtree Branches Book

STEALTHY NINJAS

ANCIENT WARRIORS

Thomas Kingsley Troupe

Crabtree Publishing
crabtreebooks.com

School-to-Home Support for Caregivers and Teachers

This high-interest book is designed to motivate striving students with engaging topics while building fluency, vocabulary, and an interest in reading. Here are a few questions and activities to help the reader build upon his or her comprehension skills.

Before Reading:
- *What do I think this book is about?*
- *What do I know about this topic?*
- *What do I want to learn about this topic?*
- *Why am I reading this book?*

During Reading:
- *I wonder why...*
- *I'm curious to know...*
- *How is this like something I already know?*
- *What have I learned so far?*

After Reading:
- *What was the author trying to teach me?*
- *What are some details?*
- *How did the photographs and captions help me understand more?*
- *Read the book again and look for the vocabulary words.*
- *What questions do I still have?*

Extension Activities:
- *What was your favorite part of the book? Write a paragraph on it.*
- *Draw a picture of your favorite thing you learned from the book.*

TABLE OF CONTENTS

In the Shadows

The ninja moves quietly along the rooftop. His footsteps are silent. Dark shadows keep him hidden from others.

He pulls a short dagger from his belt. The ninja crouches and waits to strike. When his enemy is near, he jumps down. No one ever saw the ninja's attack!

What's a Ninja?

Ninjas, also known as *shinobi*, were ancient **mercenaries** in medieval Japan. They were hired to carry out secret spying missions.

Ninja warriors were often paid by heads of armies. Their missions included gathering information, causing confusion to distract an enemy, and sometimes killing them.

Fun Fact

The full Japanese word for ninja is *shinobi-no-mono* which means "people who survive or endure."

A ninja didn't always work at night. Ninjas wore disguises to fool enemies. The disguises allowed them to gain access into enemy **strongholds**.

Because of their secret ways, many believed ninjas were **supernatural**. Some were even sure they could fly. Others thought ninjas were unstoppable fighters.

Ninja History & Life

Prince Yamato Takeru is often thought of as the first ninja. He was a Japanese folk hero, believed to have lived in 2nd century, AD.

According the legend, Yamato disguised himself as a woman. He used his costume to kill two **chieftains**. His story was passed down through the ages to inspire ninja warriors.

Ninjas usually belonged to a **clan**. Two of the main ninja clans in Japan were the Iga and Koga clans. They were named after the two Japanese regions.

These clans trained new ninjas in warfare, **espionage**, and intelligence. Little else is known about life in ninja clans. The ninja lived very secretive lives.

Fun Fact

Samurai warriors and ninjas often worked together. They hired ninjas to sneak in and spy on and kill their enemies. Though they used them, samurai thought of ninjas as a lower class of warrior.

Ninja Clothing

The popular image is of a ninja dressed all in black with a hood and mask to hide his face. But ninjas did not wear a uniform.

In movies, ninjas also appear wearing boots called *tabi*. Tabi boots are split at the end to separate the toes. But tabi are traditional Japanese footware. They were not designed specifically for ninjas or even martial arts.

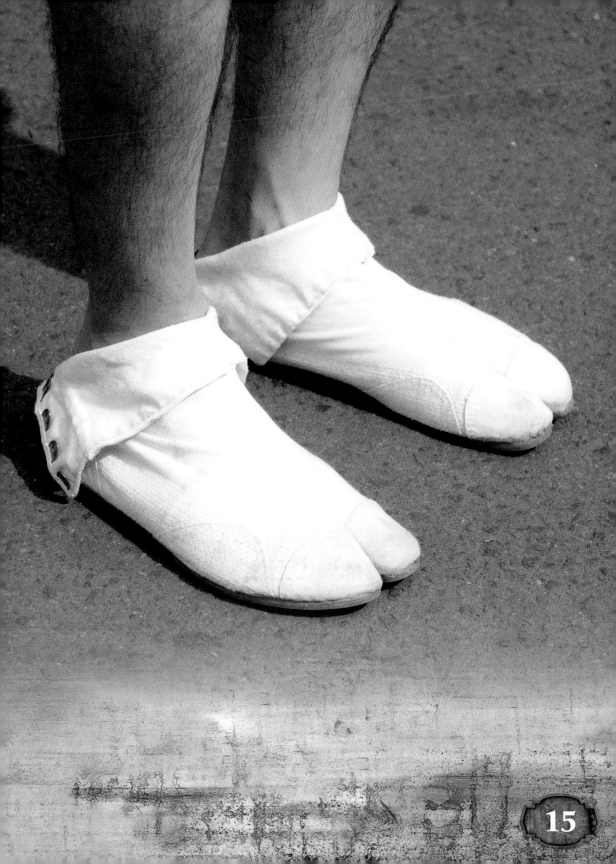

In reality, ninjas mainly wore disguises to blend in with the enemy. They could make themselves look like anyone else. A skilled ninja could hide in plain sight.

Because ninjas needed protection when in battle, many wore a light armor. The armor was made to let them move easily and not look **suspicious**.

Ninja Weapons

Although they carried few weapons, ninjas are known for the unique weapons they used. Some used a shorter version of the *katana* sword. The *o-wakazashi* sword was short and light.

Shuriken are weapons thrown by hand, such as throwing stars. Made of sharp metal, they could be deadly. Though not very accurate, shuriken were used to distract or injure enemies.

Fun Fact

Longer katanas were mostly used by samurai in medieval Japan. Since some ninjas worked closely with samurai, they added shorter katanas to their **arsenal**.

Some ninja weapons served multiple purposes. The kama looks like a farming tool. It has a curved sickle-like blade attached to a handle.

Fun Fact

Don't confuse *makibishi* for jacks you'd find on a playground! Makibishi are sharper and more dangerous. They were thrown on the ground where enemies would step on them and injure their feet.

In certain situations, attacking from a distance was best. Some ninja were trained to use a bow and arrow. Shorter bows were used in close combat and longer bows for distant targets.

Ninja Fighting

Children born into a ninja class were taught *ninjutsu*, the art of espionage. Training included disguise, **stealthy** movement, and fighting. These secrets and techniques would be passed down through generations.

For battle, ninjas were taught hand-to-hand combat. They also learned to wrestle and box to defeat enemies.

Ninjas were considered the perfect athletes of their day. They could run, jump, swim, climb walls, hike long distances, and throw weapons.

Legends spread about the abilities of ninja warriors. People began to believe they could do unbelievable things such as disappear or pass through walls like a ghost. Their best trick was to blend in with others unnoticed before striking.

Ninjas Today

Where have all the ninjas gone? The last record of ninjas fighting in battle was in the Shimabara Rebellion (1637-1638). Then Japan entered a long period of peace and the need for ninjas disappeared.

Jinichi Kawakami is a grandmaster ninja and head of the Koka clan in Iga region today. But he says the skills of the ninja have no place in the modern world.

Fun Fact

Jinichi Kawakami is considered the "last real ninja." He inherited the Koga ninja clan's scrolls when he was 18 and runs the Banke Shinobinoden ninjitsu school in Japan.

Today there are ninja museums to visit in Japan. The **agility** of the ninja in climbing and running is not unlike the athletic activity of parkour today.

Ninjas have been featured as characters in literature, comics, cartoons, and movies around the world, creating interest in their history. Ninjas will always be remembered as the stealthiest ancient warriors!

Glossary

agility (uh-JIL-i-tee) The power of moving quickly and easily

arsenal (AAR-suh-nuhl) A storehouse for weapons

chieftains (CHEEF-tnz) Leaders of a band, tribe, or clan

clan (KLAN) A group made up of households who share a common ancestor

espionage (EH-spee-uh-naazh) The practice of spying

mercenaries (MUR-suh-neh-reez) Soldiers paid to fight in an army

stealthy (STEL-thee) Slow, deliberate, and secret in action

strongholds (STRAANG-howldz) Buildings or other structures that are safe from attack

supernatural (soo-pr-NA-chr-uhl) An ability beyond or outside of nature

suspicious (suh-SPI-shuhs) Having a feeling that something is wrong

Index

Websites to Visit

www.winjutsu.com/ninjakids/

https://web-japan.org/kidsweb/explore/history/q4.html

www.youtube.com/watch?v=MMM3hVp-1Ag
[Video of the ninja's lost history]

About the Author

Thomas Kingsley Troupe is the author of over 200 books for young readers. When he's not writing, he enjoys reading, playing video games, and investigating haunted places with the Twin Cities Paranormal Society. Otherwise, he's probably taking a nap or something. Thomas lives in Woodbury, Minnesota, with his two sons.

Written by: Thomas Kingsley Troupe
Designed by: Bobbie Houser
Series Development: James Earley
Proofreader: Kathy Middleton
Educational Consultant: Marie Lemke M.Ed.

Photographs:
istock: Lise Gagne: cover, p. 1; Aleksei Mitrushkin: p. 8; 1001nights: p. 9; HunterKitty: p. 10-11; visualspace: p. 12-13, 28-29; SAND555: p. 16; Portugal2004: p. 21; YusukeYamamoto: p. 24-25
Shutterstock: dotshock: p. 4-5; metamorworks: p. 6-7, 14; Fajrul Islam: p. 15; Tedi Atmapradhana: p. 17; Viktor Gladkov: p. 18-19; MyImages - Micha: p. 20; Santiti Chanpeng: p. 21; Aleksey Mnogosmyslov: p. 22-23; Fotokvadrat: p. 26-27

Crabtree Publishing

crabtreebooks.com   800-387-7650

Copyright © 2024 Crabtree Publishing

All rights reserved. No part of this publication may be reproduced, stored in a retrieval system or be transmitted in any form or by any means, electronic, mechanical, photocopying, recording, or otherwise, without the prior written permission of Crabtree Publishing.

Printed in the U.S.A./072023/CG20230214

Published in Canada
Crabtree Publishing
616 Welland Ave.
St. Catharines, Ontario
L2M 5V6

Published in the United States
Crabtree Publishing
347 Fifth Ave
Suite 1402-145
New York, NY 10016

Library and Archives Canada Cataloguing in Publication
Available at Library and Archives Canada

Library of Congress Cataloging-in-Publication Data
Available at the Library of Congress

Hardcover: 978-1-0398-0950-5
Paperback: 978-1-0398-1003-7
Ebook (pdf): 978-1-0398-1109-6
Epub: 978-1-0398-1056-3